Historic
of
Dunstable

The
Book
Castle

Vivienne Evans

First published May 2002
by The Book Castle
12 Church Street
Dunstable
Bedfordshire

© Vivienne Evans, 2002 (text)
© Lewis Evans, 2002 (map)

With thanks for the use of their photographs to
Nigel Benson, Omer Roucoux, Lee Stanley and Bruce Turvey

ISBN 1-903747-15-5
Designed by Lee Stanley, Dunstable, Beds
Printed by Pear Tree Press Ltd, Stevenage, Herts

Front cover: detail from a nineteenth-century postcard. O. Roucoux collection

Contents

Introduction   5

     Dunstable with the Priory
     The Closing of the Priory
     Dunstable Inns during the years 1700-1838

Ten Historic Inns

     The Bull   12

     The Crown   14

     The Nag's Head   16

     The Victoria   18

     The White Swan   20

     The Saracen's Head   22

     The Priory House   24

     The Norman King   26

     The Old Palace Lodge   28

     The Old Sugar Loaf   30

Key to back cover map   32

Historic Inns of Dunstable

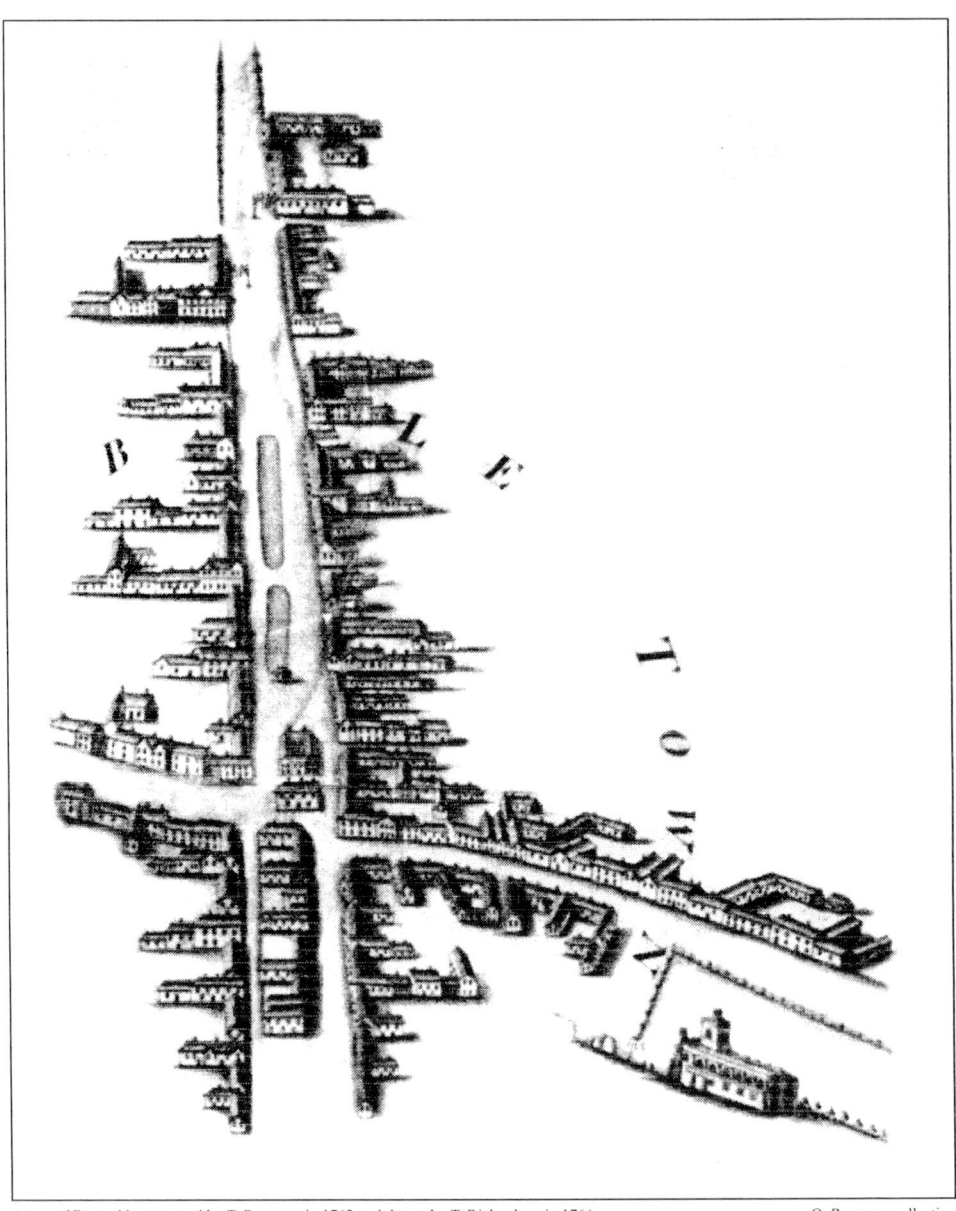

A map of Dunstable, surveyed by T. Bateman in 1762 and drawn by T. Richardson in 1766.

O. Roucoux collection

Introduction

PART I
Dunstable with the Priory

When King Henry I's advisors planted a business centre on Dunstaple's crossroads (c1106), they wanted a collection and marketing centre for agricultural produce and a safe place for travellers to break their journeys. A palace was built for Henry to use when travelling and the Augustinian Priory that he founded, opposite the palace, provided accommodation for all types of travellers. **Priory House**, which still stands today, was part of their main hostel. By the late 14th century, there were so many travellers that the prior was obliged to open or licence commercial inns. **The Saracen's Head** probably dates from this time and had **The George** as its neighbour.

The 450-acre new town had been built along the two main roads [A5 - Watling Street and A505 Icknield Way] and there was no space to build new inns, so some time before 1500, two small inns were built in the middle of North Street. **The Lyon** and **The Peacock** were included in Thomas Rowlandson's drawing of High Street North (c1800). They were always very small and by this date were more like restaurants than hotels; soon after this **The Lyon** became a private house. At the height of the coaching industry, in 1804 they were taken down as part of a road-widening scheme. Sometime before 1381, somebody, possibly William Dyve, Lord of the Manor of Sewell, built an inn, which he called **The White Swan** (later **The Red Lion**) off the end of North Street, partly blocking East (Church) Street. He later used this as part of an endowment for a religious fraternity; little is known about this inn during its early years. When the Fraternity was closed, it became part of the royal estate and, in 1578, businessman, John Griggs was renting it for £4 per year. It was obviously a high-class inn because the Earl of Huntingdon chose to stay there in 1639; he enjoyed a lavish menu including Dunstable larks. This was just before the Civil War and, in 1644, the landlord was shot dead for refusing to hand over his horses to the Royalist soldiers. The new landlord must have been a Royalist, because the next year, King Charles I called there to rest and to change horses after the Battle of Naseby. This famous inn, with its barns at the back and its tap room further down East (Church) Street, continued to run successfully until the coming of the railway. It then closed for a short time and re-opened as a commercial and family hotel. As such, it was a focal point in Dunstable life, hosting dinners, auctions, billiard evenings and many other activities. Despite its lack of space, it offered thirteen bedrooms and stabling for fourteen horses. It was demolished in 1963 as part of a road-widening programme.

By the time that the Priory closed (in 1539), its rent list noted two other, much bigger inns in North Street. On the east, **The White Hart** became one of Dunstable's main coaching inns. It stood on a large site beside what became known as White Hart or Houghton Lane. It had its own blacksmith's shop; the last tenants of this were the Nichols family, who gave their name to the present Nicholas Way. It also had a block of stables, which became cottages. In the 17th century, it was one of

Historic Inns of Dunstable

High St North plait market from the Queen magazine, Nov.9, 1861.

O.Roucoux collection

Bedfordshire's largest inns, but it closed in the late 18th century and re-opened as a popular town-centre public house. This was taken down in 1965 as preparation for the Quadrant shopping centre. **The Bear**, mentioned in the 17th century, later **The King's Arms**, was probably trading at this period as part of **The White Hart**. On the other side of the road, **The White Horse** is represented today by the stone archway. Even before the Priory closed, this inn was of such importance and luxury that King Henry VIII and his court used it. In the following century, **The White Horse** became Dunstable's first post office and the mail-coaches collected and delivered letters and parcels for the town and for villages from miles around. However, by the end of the 17th century, the inn was out of date and probably too costly to repair, so it was broken into separate units (see **The Wrestlers** and **The Anchor**).

In the 19th century, part of the site was used as a market hall (later town hall) and part became a central part of the straw-hat industry. The market hall was rebuilt as the town hall, but was pulled down in 1966. The site is now the offices of the Nationwide Building Society. Adjoining **The White Horse** to the south, **The Raven** (later **The Crown**) was probably in business as a beerhouse connected with **The White Horse**. Also at this time, opposite **The Saracen's Head** stood **The Falcon**, which, although mentioned in later deeds, disappeared long before living memory. Other inns and beerhouses in South Street mentioned when the priory's estates were handed over to the king were: another **Raven, The Pacoke (Peacock?)**, **The Angel, The Wowle** and another **Bull**, but nothing is known about these. One of them may have been connected with what became **The Blackboys**, later **The White**

6

Swan, because, although much altered, there is evidence of an earlier Tudor frame. There were also references to an unknown business called **The Lamb**, in East Street, which may be the same business, later known as **The Goat.**

PART II
The Closing of the Priory

After the closing of the Priory, there were more rather than less travellers and there was a desperate need for commercial accommodation. However, this was not a major problem because the people of Dunstable were quick to respond. It is of interest that three of the first new inns have names connected with royalty.

In 1542, the Fraternity that owned **The Swan** had a school nearby (for Houghton Regis boys) and its own headquarters, roughly where **The Winston Churchill** stands today. Within the next two or three years, they had bought a licence to turn it into an inn called **The King's Head** - later **The White Horse** (Church Street). This business changed its name around 1800. It was always small and the landlord often had a second trade eg John Franklin was the town constable. It was a popular town-centre public house renowned for its Beer and Baccy Band and for the mounting block that stood outside. When it was pulled down in 1963, the mounting block was taken for safety to Beecroft School. Also, just over the North Street boundary with Houghton Regis, another entrepreneur, who bought up Fraternity property, opened an inn called **The Prince's Arms**, later **The Red Host**, followed by **The Bull**.

It is not known when **The Crown Inn** first opened. By 1618 Mr Grigg was the owner; during the Civil War he was one of the few local Royalists. This is not today's Crown, but an important, private inn, near what is now the entrance to the Queen Eleanor shopping centre. It was intended for a high-class trade and was regularly used by the Duke of Bedford and his family. This inn had its own pond and blacksmith's forge out in the road and was always short of stabling. In the 18th century, it became part of the estate purchased to support The Chew School and for some years was known as **The Windmill & Still**. By the end of its life it was once again known as **The Crown** and was run by the owner of **The Duke of Bedford's Arms**. The coming of the railway caused it to close, but it re-opened a few years later as The Crown Hat Factory. Nearby, **The Nag's Head** also opened around 1600; its history is included below.

The will of George Briggs, which was published in 1692, included: **The Lyon**, **The Peacock**, **The Raven** and **The Goat**, all mentioned above. Unfortunately, nothing is known about the latter. He also owned **The Sugar Loaf** and **The Star.** Thomas Groom of **The Star** was buried in 1764 and the deeds of No 59 High Street South identify this building as being **The Star** in 1773 but by 1780 it had been converted to a private house. After several changes of use, it was known until recently as **The Grey House**. Another inn connected with the Briggs family was **The Leaden Porch**. It was first mentioned in 1598 but as 60 years earlier lead was reported stolen from the dismantled Dominican Friary, it may have been even older. For a few years, it was known as **The Green Man** but when, in the 18th century, the trustees of the Chew School owned it, it was called **The Maypole**. By the 19th century, it had been converted into the two shops known today as 16-18 West Street. The yard at the back is still known as Maypole Yard.

Drovers and waggoners, who needed enclosed paddocks, used a group of inns at the southern end of the town. **The Woolpack** which once stood on the west side of the road (near today's Woolpack Close), had a pond out in the road and closes (paddocks) at the back. It is not known when this closed. **The Cow and Hare** (later **The Waggon and Horses,**) was also trading well before 1700 and also had several acres of paddocks. Its large car park was once used as a stableyard. Also in this group, but over the Kensworth border, was **The Half Moon**, which had 3 acres of enclosed paddocks.

Yet another inn that may be connected with this period was **The Angel**. Nothing is known about this business, but there are occasional references from the 17th century onwards. It may have become **The Manor House**, which was replaced by Dunstable's first purpose-built post office and is now the offices of the DHSS. Rather more is known about **The Cock**, which adjoined the original Crown. For several generations it was owned by the Moreton family. It was probably more like a restaurant than an inn because the family was also skilled in leatherwork and used the yard at the back for making horse collars and saddles. In the 19th century the yard was used for making hats and it

was soon converted to use as a straw-hat factory.

PART III
Dunstable Inns During the Years 1700-1838

Early in the 18th century, high profits were to be made from the hospitality industry and c1740, businessman, Henry Swindall, opened a new private inn that he called **The Duke of Bedford's Arms**. This was in honour of Dunstable's new Lord of the Manor. Unfortunately, his inn was overtaken by events and it soon became a private house.

The period from around 1700 to 1838 saw many changes. The first long-distance coach service opened in 1657 and, by 1700, it had become popular, making Dunstable one of the busiest towns in the travel industry. Several coach companies used it as a first/last night's stop out of London, which provided work for the bed and breakfast trade as well as for victuallers. Food was needed for horses and, in addition, blacksmiths, wheelwrights, saddlers and harness-makers all made a good living. There was a market for souvenirs and the making of Dunstable bonnets grew out of these opportunities. Finally, one of the most profitable parts of the travel market was the hiring out of horses. However, during this period the travel market changed; from around 1785, first the Royal Mail and then the stagecoaches began to run an express service that changed horses every 12-15 miles. They continued travelling through the night and Dunstable lost much of its bed and breakfast trade. Then, about

8

the same time, an increasing number of Turnpike Trusts were created, greatly improving the roads; in 1710, a group of gentlemen formed a trust to collect tolls from Puddle Hill to Hockliffe. It took some years, but by the end of the 18th century, the roads were so much improved that most coaches managed to get further out of London before they had a meal stop. The result of this was that several of Dunstable's larger inns eg **The Bull** and **The White Hart**, closed down and re-opened as public houses. However, the hiring of horses was still very profitable and boosted the income of some of the inns.

By now **The White Horse** was considered old and inconvenient and the owner began to divide it into separate commercial units. First, the northern end of the building became a public house called **The Wrestlers** and then the section next to the archway became **The Anchor**. Both of these were classed as public houses. It is not known exactly when **The Wrestlers** closed and became a private house, but the owner, Henry Watts, a relation of the Bennett family, was a straw-hat manufacturer. Gradually the stable area and yard became Bennett's factory. **The Anchor** continued to trade until approximately 1894, when it became the offices of solicitors Middleton and Gutteridge. It still has a stone fireplace decorated with Tudor roses. It is now about to become **The White Horse**.

Although business dropped for the accommodation providers, there was still a demand for food and drink. It is sometimes difficult to date the opening

Circa 1900

Worthington G. Smith drawing of the crossroads

of some of the beerhouses and taverns eg **The Plume and Feather**, which closed in 1999 and is about to become a community centre for a nearby church, was throughout the 18th and early 19th centuries known as **The Black Horse**. It was a beer house and lodging house, catering for tradesmen, 'on the tramp' ie looking for work. Because, until the mid 1840s, Dunstable remained as four main roads, public houses off these four roads have to be somewhat later. However, Middle Row, which stood out as an island in South Street, had, at different times, at least six licensed premises. They were all small and changed from year to year; often the proprietor had a second trade. Possibly the oldest was **The Rose and Crown** (No.2) for which there are occasional references going back to Tudor times. In 1903, it was described as clean and in a fair state of repair but was 'very old with low roofs' and, by 1914, had become a ladies' dress shop. **The Cross Keys** (No.14) was owned in 1796 by the trustees of Frances Ashton's charity. It appears to have been a licensed grocery business. Although in 1869 it was described as a public house, by 1881 it had become a grocer's shop. **The Swan with Two Necks,** formerly **The Lion and The Lamb** (No.8-10) and **The Shoulder of Mutton** (No.6) were two of the largest buildings. The former became a lodging-house and a stopping-place for long-distance carriers and although by 1894 it was described as a commercial hotel, it gradually declined and closed in 1913. **The Shoulder of Mutton** was also a lodging-house; some of the people who stayed there were working in the local hat industry, while others were from as far away as York and Cornwall. Demand

for this type of accommodation fell and it closed in 1903. **The Britannia** (No.22) does not appear as a beerhouse until after 1800 and even then was very small. In 1893, the business came to an abrupt end following the fire that started at No.20 and ruined or severely damaged several other buildings. **The Magpie** (No.32?) is more difficult to place. There are several conflicting references, but in 1862 George Fox, saddler, at number 32, was its proprietor.

The Opening of the Luton to Birmingham Railway

The only two public houses found in the trade directory of 1839, which have not already been mentioned, are **The King's Arms** and **The Yorkshire Grey.** This was produced during the year that the opening of the London to Birmingham Railway (1838) began to damage the coach industry and Dunstable's inns. Several of the larger inns were forced to close and the proprietors of the smaller ones to look for a second form of employment. **The King's Arms** in High Street North, next to **The White Hart**, appears in the directories for about twenty years, but **The Horse and Groom (The Yorkshire Grey)** had a much longer history and a variety of names. Under its original name, its proprietor was a registered victualler. It then changed names several times, but was settled with the latter name before it closed in 1903. It stood on the corner of the little road leading to the Priory Church. From then on, there are numerous un-named beer houses, but due to the prosperity of the straw industry and the development of new roads, there were

10

soon many new names. Those on the main roads may previously have been in business selling beer in someone's kitchen (eg **Blacksmith's Arms** (next to **The Victoria**, West Street), or, as with **The Odd Fellows' Arms** (High Street South, next to Wood Street), which was also the Young family's bakery, part of another business.

In Church Street, **The Royal Oak,** previously **The Sawyers' Arms**, stood opposite the end of Priory Road, until the 1960s, with **The Royal George** nearby. **The First and Last** was a little later. Mid 19th century beerhouses in West Street included **The Ewe and Lamb**, which, until 1961, stood beside what is now St Mary's Gate, with **The Elephant and Castle** further east and **The Vine**, which became Ellis the barbers, further east again at number 7. In addition, there was, at one time, a **Wheatsheaf** where Princes Street starts today.

The Wheatsheaf, which is still trading in High Street North, opened towards the end of the 19th century and the earlier **Wheatsheaf**, in High Street South, may have been another name for the above-mentioned **Odd Fellows' Arms**. However, according to the early nineteenth century book 'Dunno's Originals', an even earlier **Wheatsheaf** once stood on the corner of High Street South and Church Street. Two other beerhouses on the east side of High Street South that opened later in the 19th century were **The Star and Garter** and **The Greyhound**. **The Highwayman** Hotel was originally The Highfields Tea Room. On the other side of the road, south of The Square, **The Carpenter's Arms**, (first licensed by a carpenter in the 1870s?), continued trading until the 1920s; it is now a dentist's surgery. **The Eight Bells**, at the other end of The Square (No.10 Ashton Street), lasted until the redevelopment that took place in 1958.

CONCLUSION

The 60 businesses mentioned in this book are only part of Dunstable's proud history of hospitality eg there are several 17th century references to **Three Black Swans**, which has not yet been identified and the importance of the wall paintings in The Nationwide Building Society, suggest that this was also an inn.

Any of the later beerhouses may have opened earlier than stated but without registering a name. A change of name can also cause confusion; in 1870, Daniel Costin registered **The Blacksmith's Arms** as **The Velocipede**. The entries in this Historic Inns of Dunstable have been restricted to the immediate town centre, before the growth of Dunstable after c1841. The later beerhouses that have been included are all on the four main roads. However, in addition to these, **The Forester's Arms**, previously **The Cock**, which, up to 1973 stood in Chapel Walk and was, for many years connected to a whiting works, may pre-date 1841. Once new streets were developed, more licensed businesses were quickly opened.

Historic Inns of Dunstable

1969   © Bruce Turvey

The coaching inn that once stood on this site was opened in the late 16th century and was called **The Prince's Arms**. It stood on the Houghton Regis side of the town boundary and, unlike the Dunstable inns, had 15½ acres of land. It was for this reason that, following his great enterprise in starting the first long-distance stagecoach from London to Shrewsbury in 1657, entrepreneur Henry Earle bought the inn (now called **The Bull**), enclosed the land and used it as one of his regional headquarters for stabling horses.

Its success was assured and by the end of the century it was not only the largest inn in Dunstable, but also one of the biggest buildings in South Bedfordshire. Not only did Earle's stagecoaches stay there overnight, but it was also used by other firms and, at the same time, managed to be popular with private travellers.

In 1744, the Earl of Egremont stayed there with his wife, as they travelled to Buxton to 'take the water'. Arthur Young, secretary to the Board of Agriculture, was delighted with the 'good mutton steaks' (cost 1s 0d/now 5p) that he enjoyed there in 1770.

The Bull

High Street North

However, Viscount Byng was not so pleased when, offered duck for supper, he remembered seeing them 'dead and dying in the orchard'!

In addition to private travellers and stagecoaches, at times The Bull unknowingly offered hospitality to highwaymen. Gentleman Harry, who, bored with his studies at Cambridge University, had robbed his way to London, using charm instead of a pistol, then came very near to capture. He left the city and rode quietly up the Holyhead Road. However, south of Dunstable, he could not resist robbing the Warrington coach before riding confidently on into Dunstable. There, he charmed his way into **The Bull** kitchen and fell asleep over a glass or two of brandy. Sometime later, he woke with a shock to hear the Warrington coach entering the yard. He escaped but was later arrested at Woburn.

In 1785, **The Bull** was still regarded as one of Dunstable's top private inns but soon afterwards, in response to the drop in demand, it closed, was rebuilt and became a popular public house. Many of the houses in north-west Dunstable are built on The Bull Closes.

September 1984   © Lee Stanley

Historic Inns of Dunstable

This is the third name used by this popular town centre inn; each one identified a different type of business. Thomas Bentley, who also owned the adjoining **White Horse Inn**, owned it in 1542. At this stage in its history, it had no name but it must have been the tap, or beerhouse, connected with **The White Horse** and used by the coachmen and servants. A hundred years later, it was known as **The Raven** and was a small independent inn whose owner made extra money by hiring out horses. The Raven Closes (paddocks) were off High Street South. Working with horses could lead to trouble with the law. In the 17th century, a horse thief stabled stolen horses there, while trying to sell them in the market.

Later, entrepreneur George Briggs, who owned six inns, bequeathed **The Raven** to his nephew, John Pratt, but by 1792 it was owned by the Lucas Brewery of Sun Street, Hitchin. By this time, it had become a town-centre tavern, selling food and drink and William Lucas renamed it **The Crow**. (There was a well-known proverb 'as black as a Dunstable crow'.) A drawing, published in 1861, shows **The Crow** sign hanging over the covered stalls of the plait market. Customers came to

14

The Crown

the market from miles around and **The Crow** was ideally placed to hire out rooms for business deals, for stabling horses and for serving food and drink. Apart from the landlord, Joseph Fearn, who was a barrel-maker, most of the landlords worked in the hat industry and provided accommodation for bonnet-sewers.

When **The** (old) **Crown Inn** closed and became a hat factory, a new beer house (now **The Borough Arms**) took

the name. So when, in 1869, Frederick Field, landlord of **The** (second) **Crown**, took on the licence of **The Crow**, he transferred the name. He was also listed as straw-hat and bonnet manufacturer. By 1894, George Ambrose Pleasant ran the successful **Crown Inn**, without the support of a second business.

July 1981   ↖ Bruce Turvey

Historic Inns of Dunstable

June 1953   © Bruce Turvey

Once the Priory Hostel was closed (1539), it was necessary to open more commercial inns, but building stopped during the Civil War. Afterwards, Josias Settle opened an inn on Dunstable crossroads. He lived there with his wife, Sarah, their four sons and a daughter, all born between 1648 and 1657. **The Nag's Head** was a typical small inn of its day, where the landlord was expected to shave his customers, cut their hair, pull their aching teeth, lance their boils and generally care for their comfort. The eldest son, Elkanah, went to Oxford University and became a famous playwright. The plays that he wrote for the queen and the pageants for the Lord Mayor of London are in the British Museum. He died in 1724 and is buried in London. His wife, Mary Warner, was daughter of a local innkeeper; Elkanah's sister, Sarah, married Mary's brother, John. When Josias died in 1667, his heir, Jeremiah, was 9 years old, so John and Sarah managed the inn for him. Elkanah's two other brothers died during Dunstable's great witch scandal.

When an old lady called Elizabeth Pratt arrived asking for toast and ale, Sarah went to fetch them while Elizabeth talked to 11 year-old John and 12 year-old

The Nag's Head
On the corner of High Street North and West Street

Josias. They quickly became critically ill and, even before they died, Josias sen. convinced himself that Elizabeth had bewitched them. He confronted her and she confessed to meeting the devil and holding covens on the Downs. More children died and also horses and pigs (anthrax?), so the magistrates sent her to Bedford gaol. Luckily, she died before prosecution.

Things settled down, new landlords came and, before the arrival of the railway, landlord James Oliver sent carriers' carts to London. This trade came to an abrupt end and, to support his family, he opened a butcher's shop. Standing outside the plait market, business soon improved; new landlords took over and, by 1870, Charles Rudland advertised himself as wine and spirit merchant, corn merchant and victualler. He not only sold food and drink but also offered 'Gillard's Spice Condiment for Cattle' and 'good, well-aired beds'! By the end of the century, as today, the landlord concentrated on offering good quality food and drink.

February 1977

© Bruce Turvey

Historic Inns of Dunstable

The tithe map published in 1840 marks the lane (not yet Icknield Street) that joined West Street to the pond and Bull Pond Lane. The street line was already built up, each house backing onto The Crow's Close (paddock). The double-fronted plot, owned by baker William Groom, had a cart entrance through to the yard and a garden at the front, on what had been part of the sheep market. His shop was on the High Street and his West Street tenant was a chair-maker, William Summerfield, who also sold beer.

The next decade was an important one for Dunstable; Queen Victoria visited in 1841, when it was just recovering from the opening of Leighton Buzzard railway station and the collapse of the coaching industry. However, in 1848, Dunstable opened its own station, the straw-bonnet business was booming and building had begun in Icknield Street and Edward Street. Public houses were needed to provide food and drink for the workmen. William Summerfield moved across the road and carrier William Minnard opened **The Victoria**.

A Bedfordshire family, keeping a respectable house, attracted hawkers and other long-distance travellers. By 1860, the town was growing rapidly and beer houses were springing up all

The Victoria

around, so the next tenant, carrier David Brown, began to develop the family trade. He advertised that he was agent for 'Scrivener's superior, refreshing Ginger Beer', which he would sell (for cash) at 1s 3d per dozen bottles. He also advertised a booth (marquee) suitable for cricket matches, tea parties or picnics on Dunstable Downs.

Meanwhile, John Vickers, a Buckinghamshire horse-breaker, had opened a business in Church Street, where his wife sold crockery and he hired out horses. Their sons went into the building trade and, by the end of the 1860s, John and his wife, Ann Marie, had moved into

The Victoria. John died in 1870 and the magistrate transferred the licence to Ann Marie, but she retired and Fullers of Woburn advertised a 'Free Spirit House'…with bar, parlour, taproom and outbuildings. They sold to J Batchelor of Dagnall, with Fred Parkhouse as tenant, paying £22 per year.

September 1984

© Lee Stanley

Historic Inns of Dunstable

This may have been opened by the Augustinian Priory, but was near enough to their boundary to have room for a stableyard and two paddocks which reached across to Inlands Lane (later Englands Lane now Britain Street.) In its early days it was known as **The Two Black Boys** but changed sometime after the earlier **White Swan** became **The Red Lion.**

This **White Swan** was valued at £120 when, in 1769, Edward Mouse sold it to John Gibson. It remained in private hands until 1782 when Thomas Godfrey Burr was expanding the family's new Luton brewery. The inn was small with a business much as today but, as the coach industry grew, the landlords used their land. In 1843, five years after the station was built at Leighton Buzzard, Deacon's Express Waggons were still changing horses there, every night and morning, on their way to and from London and Leeds. On alternate days, The Deliance stagecoach called in on its journies to and from Manchester. However this important trade was ending and **The Swan** was bought by the successful brewers, Simpsons of Baldock. William Gilbert, the landlord who had built up the coaching side of the business, now adapted it for a more

The White Swan

High Street South

local trade. Standing at the end of the market place he was ideally situated to let out his stables and to provide good food and drink for visiting farmers. He laid out a skittles alley and encouraged visits from local residents and workers in the hat and building industries.

However by 1851 Gilbert, who only had his niece (whom he had brought from Kent) and a twelve-year-old boy to help him, was in his seventies. At this time Dunstable landlords needed a second trade and, for some years, William Nichols, Signwriter, and later Frederick Young, Whiting manufacturer, were the licensees. Although there was a period of neglect at the end of the century, **The White Swan** was in good repair and ready to become a successful town centre public house in the 20th century.

© Lee Stanley

Historic Inns of Dunstable

Circa 1905   O. Roucoux collection

This inn was opened by the Augustinian Priory when their hostel (Priory House) could no longer accommodate all the pilgrims and other travellers passing through. Like Priory House, which was built in the late 13th century, it is two steps below street level. There were so many travellers that between this inn and their gatehouse, another opened called **The George**. By the 17th century, another inn, called **The Bell** had been built in-between. Their names reflect their history; travellers to the Holy Land were fearful of attack by the Saracens, St George of England was canonised in 1222 and the Priory bells were just across the meadow.

At first the inns had separate owners; in 1542 the king's steward paid £4 per year for **The Saracen's Head** and William Chambers paid over £3 for **The George**. By the mid 17th century, Josias Settle of **The Nag's Head** owned **The Bell** and a city businessman owned the other two. It is said that a royalist landlord buried gold coins under his stable floor, which were discovered after a fire in 1815.

The Saracen's Head

High Street South

By the 18th century, only **The Saracen's Head** remained open; it had a pond in the road by the front door plus a blacksmith's forge, barns and a cottage. It was leased by a family of bricklayers, whose wives ran the licensed business. In 1791, when the coaching industry was expanding, a widowed daughter, Hannah Cook, enlarged the building and business, ready for James Cook to act as agent for the Leeds Express, the Manchester Defiance, the Liverpool Star, the Birmingham Tally-Ho and several long-distance carriers. The new railway forced the inn to close but it re-opened as a commercial hotel and became agent for the Midland Railway.

Later they installed petrol pumps and an inspection pit and welcomed touring groups of motorcars, motorbikes and bicycles. Standing near the cattle market, it provided stabling and special lunches for farmers, cricket club teas and popular dinners for the bell-ringers and other town societies.

March 2002 © Lee Stanley

Historic Inns of Dunstable

1982   © O.Roucoux

While staying in Dunstable during 1109, King Henry I arranged for Augustinian canons from Colchester to open a house in London. When they had finished, Henry asked them to open a third house - The Priory of St Peter, Dunstaple.

Each canon was an ordained clergyman and would pray for King Henry. They were not strictly enclosed and could run his new town and provide accommodation for travellers. Royal parties and bishops stayed with the prior, poor travellers in the almonry and the sick in the hospital, but the majority of travellers stayed in **The Hostel** - now

Priory House. The prior recognised the importance of the hosteller. The canon chosen had to be able to converse with both gentlemen and ladies, and supply food and drink, plus cups, spoons, towels, bedding, a candle and a good fire.

Priory House outlasted the canons' departure in 1540 because Henry VIII originally planned a new cathedral. Unable to afford it, he made Richard Greenway, from Aylesbury, 'Keeper of the Mansion and Gardens'. Later, it passed to Sir Leonard Chamberlain MP and from him to a Dunstable family. In 1590, Elizabeth Ames, describing the house in her will, included a big hall,

24

The Priory House

High Street South

open to the roof, with a central fireplace, a parlour, lined with wainscot, and a bedroom, lined with painted cloths.

After the Civil War, Dr Robert Crawley MD (of Someries, Luton) bought the Mansion House and '5 acres called by the name of The Pryory'. His grandson, Dr Thomas Crawley, treated patients with nervous diseases as paying guests, mixing kindness, good food and medicine. After he died, in 1752, it frequently changed hands until, in the 1830s, London hat manufacturers, Munt and Brown, opened a factory employing 200 bonnet-sewers. Their manager, Samuel Collis, lived in Priory House with his wife and nine children. The factory closed c1907 (part of the wall is still visible today) and Mr and Mrs Munt lived in Priory House. In the mid 20th century, it became Dunstable Council's offices, then commercial offices, before re-opening in a hospitality role in the new millenium.

June 1989 © Bruce Turvey

Historic Inns of Dunstable

Circa 1955

Around 1106 King Henry I ordered a palace to be built as part of his new town of Dunstaple. Made up of a series of 'houses' built around a great courtyard, it stood on a nine-acre site. It was finished in time for him to entertain a large party at Kingsbury in 1109. Both King Henry and later King Stephen used it for a great Christmas Court.

In 1204, King John gave to the Augustinian Priory the site and garden where King Henry I 'once had houses'. The Prior let it out to wealthy Dunstable wool merchants who could use the out-houses as a wool yard. Wool merchant John Durrant was one of the wealthiest men in Bedfordshire but, following his death in 1297, Kingsbury fell into disrepair. However, in 1329, it was repaired for the young King Edward III to host a great tournament. This tilting-yard type of tournament was probably held in the courtyard.

By 1542, George Cavendish had bought Kingsbury and he was renting 'The Great Croft' between Kingsbury and North Street. This later became known as Walnut Close.

By 1600, Kingsbury was owned by William Marshe, whose family had farmed part of Caddington and Kensworth. Some of his descendents

The Norman King

On the corner of Church Street and Kingsway

developed Kingsbury Farm, others became connected with the City of London; their monuments are in the Priory Church. Between them they founded the Ladies Lodge, the Cart and Ashton almshouses and the Chew School. Income from the Ashton Almshouses was used to found the Ashton Schools. William's son, Francis, married Rebecca, of the inn-keeping Briggs family. His grandson, Doctor John Marshe, married Dorothy Wolsley, cousin of the 17th century traveller and writer, Celia Fiennes, who visited her at Kingsbury. It later became a commercial farm but in 1925, local businessman William Bagshawe converted it back into a gentleman's residence. Two years later, he turned the barn, which became **The Norman King**, into the Town Museum; this lasted for 7 years. In 1935, twelve acres of the farm were sold for the Kingscroft Estate.

Around 1960, the estate was broken up; one end became the home of Dr. and Mrs Ashton, the other, **The Old Palace Lodge** Hotel. Flowers Brewery bought the barn and, using contemporary materials, they enlarged it and, in October 1961, opened **The Norman King**.

Historic Inns of Dunstable

June 1984   © Nigel Benson

King Henry I came to the throne in 1100 and for 6 years continued the violent quarrel previously waged between his eldest brother Robert and his deceased brother William II. He captured Robert in 1106 and so became undisputed king of England and Duke of Normandy. Wanting to develop national and international trade he planted a business centre on Dunstaple crossroads; to encourage this and, to provide a royal presence, he had a palace built and installed a 'housekeeper' (steward).

Kingsbury Palace was finished and furnished ready for a royal visit in 1109. From then on there were numerous royal visits, the most important being Henry's and Stephen's Christmas courts, and the peace conference between King Stephen and the future King Henry II. When the building got older and more costly to maintain, King John gave it to the Augustinian Priory but there were later informal visits and in 1329 it hosted a royal tournament. Just before the Dissolution, Sir Thomas Wolsey's secretary, George Cavendish, bought it. In 1525 he was president of the prestigious Dunstable Fraternity.

By 1600, William Marshe and his wife Elizabeth were living at Kingsbury and their three surviving children grew up

The Old Palace Lodge
Church Street

there. They were a family of benefactors and their monuments are in Priory Church. The youngest, Francis, married Rebecca Briggs from the wealthy inn owning family. His older brother, John, married Blandina Iremonger, daughter of a Leighton Buzzard lawyer. Their daughter, another Blandina, started the nearby 'Ladies Lodge' almshouses. Francis's sister Elizabeth married wealthy businessman Thomas Chew and their son, William, left money to start the respected Chew School; the daughters, Francis and Jane, both married distillers and as widows they both founded almshouses. Spare income from Francis Ashton's bequest was used to start the two Ashton Schools.

There were many changes during the 19th century and Kingsbury became a farmhouse. In 1959, wealthy businessman Arthur Bagshaw sold the eastern end to Creasey Hotels. In 1960 it opened as **The Old Palace Lodge** Hotel. It was later owned by Andrew Weir Hotels and, in 1999, was purchased by Hanover International Hotels.

March 2002 © Lee Stanley

Historic Inns of Dunstable

Circa 1910   O.Roucoux collection

The **Sugar Loaf**, built to meet the expanding travel and tourism business following the Restoration in 1660, was opened by the wealthy Briggs family, relations of the Marshes of Kingsbury. Jane Cart of Kingsbury bought it c1717 to help to support the Chew School. She had it partly rebuilt, but **The Sugar Loaf Tap**, now a shop, was not built until 1850. The inn was about the same size as Kingsbury, but built with three storeys, to leave room for stables, outhouses and paddocks. Its main income was from the hiring out of horses; these were of such fine quality that they were a tourist attraction and brought visitors to the town.

A very respectable couple, John and Jane Lee were chosen as landlords and when John died, first Jane and then her daughter-in-law Eleanor took over; they built up a very high class business. Their horses were in great demand and for many years **The Sugar Loaf** was the post office for South Bedfordshire. The 1830 receipt book (on show today) includes the names of numerous lords and ladies, as well as bishops, judges and army officers.

In the 1830s, travellers were charged 4s 0d (20p) for bed and breakfast, plus an extra 1s 0d for a fire and 2s 0d for

The Old Sugar Loaf

candles. Tea with bacon and egg or ale with Welsh Rarebit cost another 2s 0d. Families carrying home the body of a loved one were charged 10s 6d (52½p) for 'a room for the corpse', plus 4s 6d (22½p) for 'refreshments for sitter-up'. However, its continued success depended on its ability to attract local trade, eg landowners who slept there while waiting for a coach, or on their way to London. The Duke of Bedford's steward held the manor court there and gave the tenants beer and sandwiches. The trustees of the almshouses met there and gave 'the old ladies' an annual dinner of mutton and caper sauce, followed by plum pudding, pies and pastries. When coaches gave way to trains, **The Sugar Loaf** Commercial and Family Hotel became an agent for the railway and, at a later period, replaced the stables with petrol pumps. For the mayor's banquet in 1874, the chef provided mock turtle soup followed by courses of fish, poultry, game, a wide choice of pies and puddings and a dessert of fruit and nuts. From then on, most Dunstable societies went to **The Sugar Loaf** for their annual dinners.

July 1972   © Bruce Turvey

Historic Inns of Dunstable

key to back cover map

Number	Location	Latest Name	Previous Name
1	High St North W	Bull	Red Hart, Prince's Arms
2		Angel	
3		Crown	Windmill and Still, Crown
4		Cock	
5		White Horse)	Wrestlers
6		White Horse)	Anchor
7		White Horse)	Townhall
8		Crown	Crow, Raven
9		Nag's Head	
10	High St North C	Peacock	
11		Lyon	Black Lyon
12	West St N	Plume and Feather	Black Horse
13		Wheatsheaf	
14	West St S	Victoria	
15		Blacksmith's Arms	
16		Elephant and Castle	
17		Ewe and Lamb	
18	.	Vine	
19	Middle Row	Rose and crown	
20		Shoulder of Mutton	Lyon and Lamb
21		Swan with Two Necks	
22		Cross Keys	
23		Brittania	
24		Magpie	
25	Ashton Square	Eight Bells	
26	High St South W	Falcon	
27		The Clifton Arms	
28		Carpenter's Arms	
29		Woolpack	
30	High Street South E	Greyhound	
31		Froth and Elbow	Waggon and Horses
32		Star and Garter	
33		White Swan	Two Black Boys
34		Down Town Cafe	Spencer's(Grey House), Star
35		Duke's Head	Odd Fellows
36		Saracen's Head)	Saracen's Head
37		Saracen's Head)	Bell
38		Saracen's Head)	George
39		Priory House	
40		Black Lion	
41	Church St S	Wheatsheaf	
42		Lamb	Goat
43		Horse and Groom	Yorkshire Grey
44		First and Last	
45	Church St N	(Royal) George	
46		Royal Oak	Sawyer's Arms
47		Norman King	
48		Old Palace Lodge	
49		White Horse	King's Head
50		Red Lion Tap	
51	High St North E	Red Lion	White Swan
52		White Hart	
53		King's Arms	Bear (?)
54		Sugar Loaf Tap	
55		Old Sugar Loaf	
56		Duke of Bedford's Arms	
57		Wheatsheaf	